SCRUMPTIOUS SCRIPTURES

Reproducible Bible Activities

Ages 6-10

by **Lynne Lepley**

Rainbow Publishers®

www.rainbowpublishers.com

This book is dedicated to Katie Moose, who inspires me with her creativity.
My thanks also to my husband, Ralph, for his encouragement and support.

SCRUMPTIOUS SCRIPTURES FOR AGES 6-10
©2006 by Rainbow Publishers, sixth printing
ISBN 10: 1-885358-47-4
ISBN 13: 978-1-885358-47-9
Rainbow reorder #36822

Rainbow Publishers
P.O. Box 70130
Richmond, VA 23255
www.rainbowpublishers.com

Illustrator: Nancy Heard

Scriptures are from the *Holy Bible: New International Version*
(North American Edition), copyright ©1973, 1978, 1984 by
the International Bible Society. Used by permission of
Zondervan Bible Publishers.

Printed in the United States of America

Table of Contents

Introduction ———————————————————

no matter how hard we try, Bible lessons with children are often overshadowed by the excitement of a simple snack. Toss some graham crackers on the table and watch your students come to life! Fortunately, God wants us to experience Him with all of our being, so why not use the sense of taste He gave us to teach His Word?

Scrumptious Scriptures will help you lead 30 exciting lessons centered on simple snacks — providing a consistent, complete classroom experience for you and your students. Or, use the lessons as additions to your curriculum for fun ways to present Bible-based snacks. Choose from popular Old and New Testament Bible stories as well as holidays.

Each lesson includes:
- Memory Verse — relevant, age-based scripture
- You Will Need — complete list of items needed for the lesson
- Before Class — instructions and hints to prepare your lesson
- Share and Discuss — suggestions for interactive Bible storytime
- Edible Lesson — step-by-step guide to creating the snack
- Prayer — themed blessing
- Activity — easy projects using reproducible sheets that continue the lesson theme

If you do not have access to cooking areas near your classroom, simply look for this symbol

at the top of each lesson introductory page, which means no classtime cooking or special refrigeration is needed.

Those that require in-class cooking or refrigeration have this symbol

The purpose of each lesson is to allow the children to be nourished not only by the snack but also by the "soul food" you provide in Bible-teaching. May God bless you as you instruct children in the discovery of God's Word in new and fun ways.

Note: Special care should be taken when children are present during cooking and cutting. Be sure to have plenty of adult helpers to assist you and your children.

In the Beginning

Memory Verse

In the beginning God created the heavens and the earth.
~Genesis 1:1

You Will Need:

* fruit, assorted
* napkins
* animal crackers
* page 9, duplicated
* white poster board
* paper fasteners
* scissors
* crayons or markers
* scissors or craft knife

Before Class

1. Slice and prepare the fruit for eating. Any types of fruit are appropriate.

2. Copy page 9 for each child plus one extra.

3. Use the extra copy of the pattern to cut two poster board circles for each child.

4. Use the pattern again to cut out a section from one of each set of poster board circles.

Share and Discuss

Ask, **Where did the world come from?** Let the children respond. Relate the events of the six days of God's creation, then say, **God created the world out of nothing at all. Can you create something out of nothing?** Stress that only God can create something out of nothing. Then say, **God spoke the world into being. God's Word is powerful. Can you think of other examples of the power of God's Word?** If the students do not respond, hold up your Bible and remind them that it is God's Word and it has the power to change lives. Next, say, **For six days God labored, and on the seventh day He rested to enjoy all that He had made. What would happen if you never had any days off from school? How would you feel if you never stopped to worship God and thank Him?** Let the children share their thoughts. Remind them that God made the seventh day, the day of rest, to be a holy day.

Edible Lesson:

1. Offer the blessing for the snack.

2. Say, **God created everything in the world — every animal, every plant and us! God created us to need food in order to live. Our snack today reminds us of all the good things that God has given us to enjoy.**

3. Let the children help themselves to napkins and the fruit you prepared.

4. Ask, **When and how did God create plants?** Read Genesis 1:11-13.

5. Serve the animal crackers.

6. Ask, **What do you remember about the creation of animals?** Read Genesis 1:20-24.

Activity: Creation Story Wheel

1. Distribute a copy of page 9 to each child.

2. Distribute crayons or markers and encourage the children to color the pictures.

3. As the children work, talk about the illustration of the six days of creation.

4. Give each child a set of two poster board circles, one with the cut-out wedge.

5. Using scissors or a craft knife, make a hole in the center of each child's colored wheel. Use this as a guide to make a hole in the center of both poster board circles.

6. Help each child write the memory verse on the poster board circle with the cut-out wedge.

7. On the back of the whole circle, have the students write: "On the seventh day God rested from His work."

8. Help the children assemble the wheel by sandwiching the colored circle between the others. The circle with the cut-out wedge should be on top.

9. Distribute paper fasteners. Help the children fasten their wheels together loosely so that the top poster board circle turns to reveal the six days of creation.

Creation Story Wheel

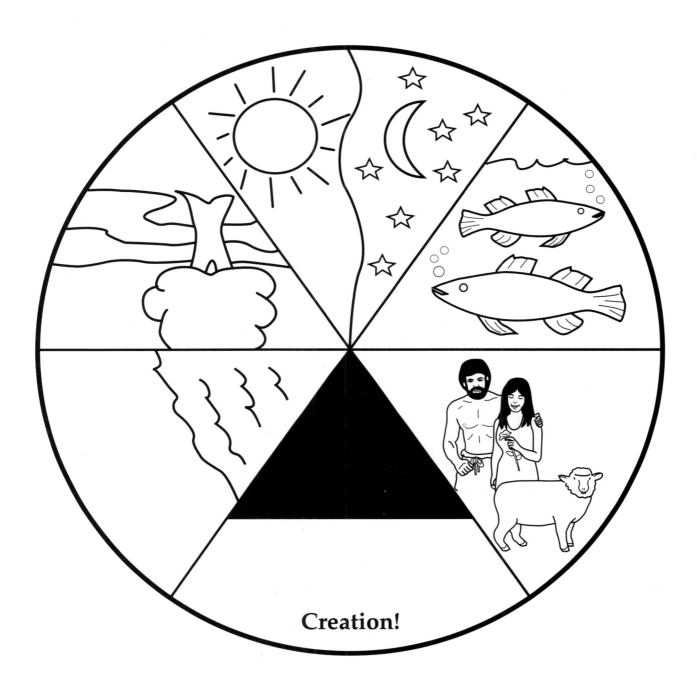

Creation!

Mud and Straw

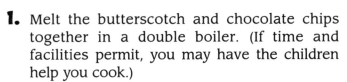

Memory Verse

This is what the Lord, the God of Israel, says: "Let my people go." ~Exodus 5:1

You Will Need:

* ✱ double boiler
* ✱ cook top
* ✱ chocolate chips
* ✱ butterscotch chips
* ✱ spoon
* ✱ chow mein noodles
* ✱ waxed paper
* ✱ page 12, duplicated
* ✱ crayons or markers

Before Class

1. Melt the butterscotch and chocolate chips together in a double boiler. (If time and facilities permit, you may have the children help you cook.)

2. Remove the mixture from the heat and stir in chow mein noodles.

3. Spoon the treats onto the waxed paper.

4. Allow the snacks to cool before eating.

5. Make a copy of page 12 for each child.

6. Reread Exodus 1-4 to refresh your memory about the Israelites' oppression by Pharaoh.

Share and Discuss

Discuss slavery with the children. Help them to understand that slaves were not free to do as they wish — they were forced to do whatever their master ordered them to do and they were often mistreated. Say, **Pharaoh, the Egyptian king, was very cruel to the Israelites. Two Israelites, Moses and Aaron, confronted Pharaoh. This was a courageous thing for them to do, but God gave them the courage. When they confronted Pharaoh, he got even more angry. Pharaoh took his anger out on his slaves and forced them to work harder than ever. They had to gather their own straw for bricks.** (Explain that in Bible times, mud mixed with straw was shaped into bricks and dried in the sun.) Say, **But God had the last word. God promised Moses that He would make Pharaoh let the Israelites go. God always keeps His promises.**

Edible Lesson:

1. Offer a blessing for the snack.

2. Say, **The Israelites were forced to make bricks as slaves in Egypt. This was very hard work. Our snack today reminds us of how the Israelites suffered as slaves in Egypt. See how it looks like mud and straw bricks? It also reminds us that God promised that He would not let them remain as slaves.**

3. Serve the snack on waxed paper.

Let my people go!

Activity: Moses, Aaron and Pharaoh

1. Give each child a copy of page 12.

2. Discuss what is happening in the picture. Ask, **How do you think Moses and Aaron felt as they stood before Pharaoh? How do you think Pharaoh felt to have these Israelite men speaking so harshly to him?**

3. Distribute crayons or markers.

4. Have the children draw appropriate faces and hair on Pharaoh (angry), Aaron and Moses (serious).

5. Help the children fill in the voice balloon with what Moses said to Pharaoh ("Let my people go!").

Moses, Aaron and Pharaoh

This is what the Lord, the God of Israel, says: "Let my people go."
Exodus 5:1

The Exodus

Memory Verse

Because the Lord kept vigil that night to bring them out of Egypt, on this night all the Israelites are to keep vigil to honor the Lord for the generations to come. ~Exodus 12:42

You Will Need:

* matzo, crackers or other unleavened bread
* page 15, duplicated
* crayons or markers

Before Class

1. Obtain some unleavened bread. Most larger grocery stores include a Jewish food section that carries matzo. Crackers are suitable if nothing more authentic is available.

2. Duplicate page 15 for each child.

Share and Discuss

Tell the story of the plagues that God sent to Pharaoh and Egypt as punishment and persuasion to let the Israelites go (Exodus 7-11; 12:31-42). Say, **The plague of the firstborn finally persuades Pharaoh to order the Israelites to leave. The people pick up everything and flee in the middle of the night. How would you like to be awakened in the middle of the night to discover that you have to walk on a long journey?** Explain that Jewish people have a special celebration to remember this night, called Passover. Say, **They remember how God's plagues passed over them, and how God freed them from slavery in Egypt. The Israelites had lived in Egypt for 430 years and for many of those years they had been slaves. They waited a long time for freedom, but God was faithful. God will also be faithful to us, even if we become impatient in our waiting.**

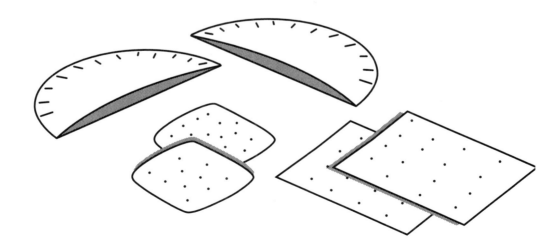

Edible Lesson:

1. Offer a blessing for the snack.

2. Explain that the Israelites left so quickly that there was no time to prepare food. Say, **The women did not have time to prepare their bread dough with yeast to make it rise. Then later on their journey they baked bread from the unleavened dough. The bread was hard and flat. To this day, when the Jews celebrate Passover they eat only unleavened bread to remind them of how God delivered them from slavery. Today we will have a snack of unleavened bread to remind us of God's love for His people, and for us.**

3. Show the children the matzo, if you have it. Explain that this is the special unleavened bread that Jews eat during Passover.

4. Remind the children that the matzo, (or crackers or unleavened bread) has the same ingredients as soft bread (flour and water) only without yeast and that is why it is hard.

Prayer:

God, thank You for our simple snack of unleavened bread because it reminds us of the wonderful thing You did in freeing the Israelites from slavery. As we eat, help us to remember that You are watching over us also. In Jesus' name we pray. Amen.

Activity: God Delivers His People

1. Distribute a copy of page 15 to each child.

2. Talk about the picture. Ask, **How must the Israelites have felt to finally be free?**

3. Distribute crayons or markers.

4. Encourage the children to draw joyful expressions on the faces of the Israelites and to draw dough in the women's dough bowls.

5. Have the children color their pictures.

God Delivers His People

God used Moses and Aaron to bring freedom to His people after many years in slavery. Draw in the faces of the people to show how they felt at being free. Draw dough in the women's bowls for the unleavened bread to show their haste in leaving.

Because the Lord kept vigil that night to bring them out of Egypt, on this night all the Israelites are to keep vigil to honor the Lord for the generations to come. Exodus 12:42

God Cares for Elijah

Memory Verse

The ravens brought him bread and meat in the morning and bread and meat in the evening, and he drank from the brook. ~1 Kings 17:6

You Will Need:

* chocolate pudding
* raisins
* chocolate ice cream cones, pointed ends
* small bowls
* spoons
* page 18, duplicated
* scissors
* crayons or markers
* string
* clear tape

Before Class

1. Purchase or prepare chocolate pudding.

2. Carefully break away the ice cream cones until they are about 1" high. (This will be the raven's beak.)

3. Crush the rest of the cones to make crumbs for the snack.

4. Copy page 18 for each child.

Share and Discuss

The story of Elijah in the wilderness is a lesson about God's faithfulness. Say, **God wants us to always be obedient to Him. Are there ever times when it is hard to obey God?** Let the children respond. Encourage them to talk about times when they have been hesitant to do what God wants them to do. Say, **God commanded Elijah to do something that might have been scary.** Tell the story of how Elijah obeyed God's command to go out into the wilderness during a time of terrible drought which was to last for several years (1 Kings 17:1-6). Say, **Without God, it would have been scary to be out in the wilderness without food or water. But God promised to take care of Elijah — and God was true to His promise! What are some of the ways God takes care of you?** Help the children to see that God uses their families, church family and others to care for their needs.

Edible Lesson:

1. Offer the blessing for the snack.

2. Say, **Elijah was completely dependent on God to supply His food and water. We depend on God for all of our needs. Our snack today reminds us that God took care of Elijah and He also takes care of us.**

3. Sprinkle ice cream cone crumbs into the bottom of each child's bowl.

4. Spoon pudding into the bowls.

5. Distribute raisins and one ice cream cone end per child.

6. Show how to use two raisins for eyes and the cone end for a beak to make the face of the raven in the pudding.

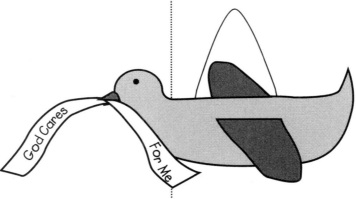

Activity: Raven Reminder

1. Give each child a copy of page 18.

2. Distribute crayons or markers.

3. Have the children color the raven's body and wings.

4. Distribute scissors.

5. Have the children cut out the body, wings and banner.

6. Help each child cut out the slot as indicated on the body of the raven.

7. Show how to slide the raven's wings into place through the slot. Secure with tape.

8. Have the students write "God Cares for Me" on the banner. Help them tape the banner to the raven's beak.

9. Tape a length of string to the back of the raven for hanging.

Raven Reminder

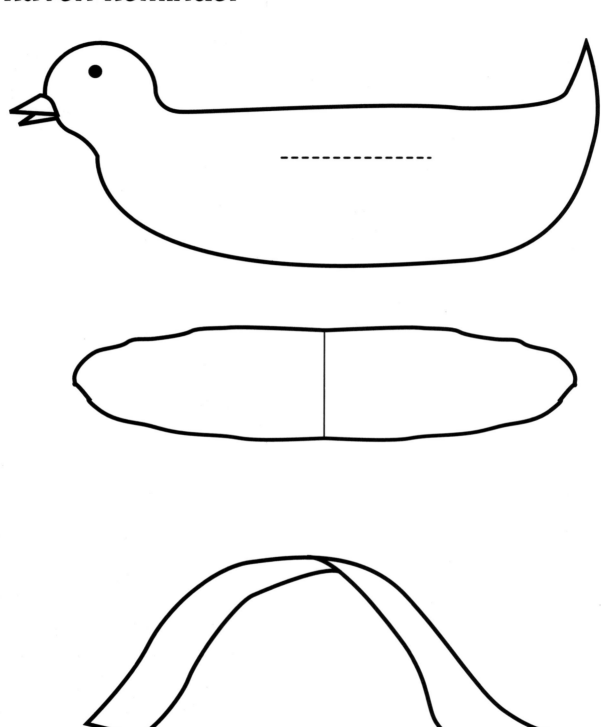

God Provides

Memory Verse

For the jar of flour was not used up and the jug of oil did not run dry, in keeping with the word of the Lord spoken by Elijah. ~1 Kings 17:16

You Will Need:

* two bowls
* measuring cup and spoons
* flour
* baking powder
* sugar
* salt
* milk
* one egg
* vegetable oil
* griddle or frying pan
* jelly or jam
* small plates
* forks
* page 21, duplicated
* crayons or markers

Before Class

1. You may either make the cakes before class (see instructions on p. 20) or have the students assist you in making them. The recipe makes about twelve 4" cakes.

2. Copy page 21 for each child.

Share and Discuss

Ask, **Can you trust a person who tells you something and then does not do it? How about someone who makes a promise and then keeps it?** Let the children respond. Say, **God proved His trustworthiness in tough situations to Elijah.** As you continue to tell the story of Elijah from 1 Kings 17:7-16, remind the children that Elijah knew God would take care of him because He had taken care of him before. Say, **Elijah knew that God would keep His word, even when it seemed impossible. Elijah told the widow to obey God without fear. The widow obeyed and used her little bits of flour and oil to make a cake, even though she was sure that she and her son would soon starve from lack of food. Imagine how amazed she must have been to discover that the flour and the oil never ran out for as long as she, her son and Elijah needed it. Nothing is impossible for God!**

Edible Lesson:

1. Offer the blessing for the snack.

2. Say, **God provided for Elijah and the widow and her son. They discovered that God never runs out of anything. Our snack today reminds us of how God provided for Elijah and his friends, and how He also provides for us.**

3. Combine in a mixing bowl: one cup of flour, two teaspoons of baking powder, two tablespoons of sugar and a pinch of salt.

4. In the other bowl, mix together: one cup of milk, one egg and two tablespoons of vegetable oil.

5. Pour the milk mixture into the dry ingredients and mix them together to make a batter.

6. Heat the griddle or frying pan and fry the batter into 4" cakes.

7. Serve the cakes on plates with jelly or jam topping.

Prayer:

God, thank You for our snack. It reminds us of how You cared for Elijah, the widow and her son — and it reminds us that You provide for our needs, also. In Jesus' name we pray. Amen.

Activity: He Provides for Me

1. Give each child a copy of page 21.

2. Talk about the pictures and how they show ways that God provides for the needs of His people.

3. Distribute crayons or markers.

4. Encourage the children to color the pictures that show a way that God provides for them. They should color all of the pictures.

5. Have the students write the memory verse on the sheet before taking it home.

He Provides for Me

God provides for our needs in many ways. Color the pictures which show ways God cares for us.

Queen Esther

Memory Verse

You Will Need:

* cookie dough
* baking sheets
* oven
* jam or jelly
* napkins
* page 24, duplicated
* craft sticks
* crayons or markers
* scissors
* glue

Before Class

1. Prepare or purchase cookie dough. Slice it into cookie-size pieces and place them on baking sheets.
2. Make one set of story puppets according to the Activity directions on p. 23 to use in Share and Discuss.
3. Reread Esther's story from the Bible (Esther 1-10) and practice telling the story.
4. Copy page 24 for each child.

Share and Discuss

Use your story puppets to talk about Esther. There are three situations to highlight: 1. If the king disposed of Queen Vashti for saying "no," what will he do to Esther when she opposes his decree to have all Jews destroyed? Esther reminds us to be kind and courteous. 2. When the king decides to honor Mordecai, Haman thinks that he is the one who will be honored so he devises a grand reward. Haman is shocked to find that his enemy Mordecai is the honoree and Haman has to carry it out. Haman's plot to destroy Mordecai ends in his own destruction. Haman reminds us that if we set out to hurt others, we may be the one who is hurt instead. 3. Mordecai is a faithful man. He is faithful to his cousin Esther. He stands up against those who would plot against the king. But most importantly, he is faithful to God in his refusal to bow down to Haman. Say, **By their actions Esther and Mordecai were examples of obedience to God. Your actions tell everyone whether or not you love God.**

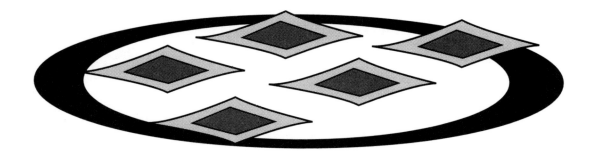

Edible Lesson:

1. Offer the blessing for the snack.

2. Say, **Jews celebrate the courage of Queen Esther in a feast known as Purim. When the story is told, everyone makes noises when Haman's name is mentioned. A sweet treat called "Haman's Ears" is also eaten. Today we will make "Haman's Ears" for our snack to remind us of Esther and Mordecai's love for God.**

3. Let the children pinch the dough at the corners to make "ears."

4. Bake the cookies according to the recipe or package instructions.

5. Remove the cookies from the oven and allow them to cool.

6. Before eating, distribute napkins and have the children put jam or jelly in their "ear cookies."

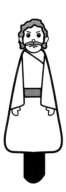

Activity: Story Puppets

1. Give each child a copy of page 24.

2. Have the children identify each puppet and tell something about them that they remember from the story of Esther.

3. Distribute crayons or markers and have the children color their puppets.

4. Distribute scissors so the children can cut out their puppets.

5. Give each child four craft sticks.

6. Show how to glue a stick to the back of each puppet body from top to bottom.

7. Encourage the children to use their puppets to tell the story of Esther to one another.

Story Puppets

Queen Esther

King Xerxes

Mordecai

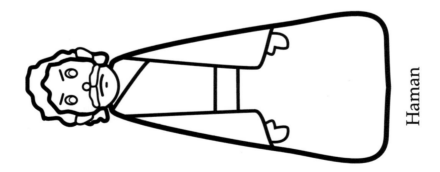

Haman

The Lord Is My Shepherd

Memory Verse

The Lord is my shepherd, I shall not be in want.
~Psalm 23:1

You Will Need:

* white sheet cake
* icing, green and brown
* canned whipped topping
* plastic knives or spreaders
* page 27, duplicated
* pencils or markers
* crayons

Before Class

1. Purchase or bake a sheet cake. Do not ice it.

2. Purchase or prepare brown (chocolate) and green icing. You can make green icing by adding green food coloring to white icing.

3. Duplicate page 27 for each child.

Share and Discuss

Say, **The memory verse is a psalm written by David. As a young boy, David was a shepherd who protected and took care of a flock of sheep. He was even willing to face danger for the sake of the sheep.** Read the memory verse. Let the children talk about the different ways a shepherd can care for sheep. Say, **Sheep need someone to watch over them. They cannot take care of themselves.** Help the children to see that we are "sheep" who cannot survive without God, our shepherd.

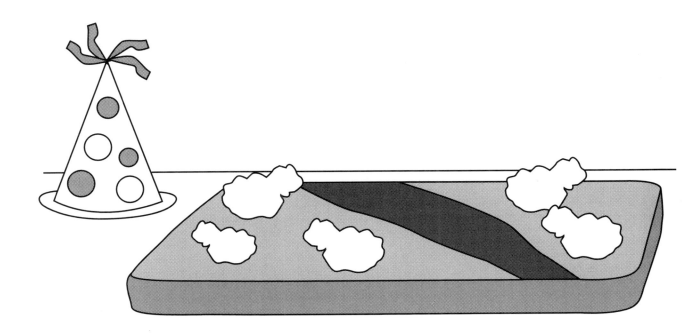

Edible Lesson:

1. Offer the blessing for the snack.

2. Say, **The Lord is our shepherd. God takes care of us in ways that we cannot take care of ourselves. Our snack today reminds us that we are God's special sheep.**

3. Make sure that the sheet cake is sufficiently cooled.

4. Place the cake so that it is accessible to all of the children. They may need to take turns so that everyone can reach the cake.

5. Provide green icing for them to put on the cake as the "pasture."

6. Provide brown icing to make a "path of righteousness" through the green icing.

7. Allow them to use the canned whipped topping to create the sheep on the scene.

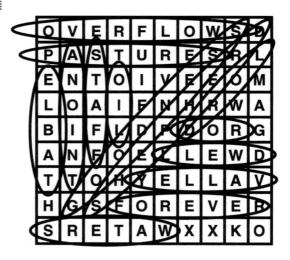

Activity: Psalm 23 Word Search

1. Distribute a copy of page 27 and pencils or markers. Talk about what the words in the list mean and how they are related to David and to God's care for us.

2. Help the children find the words in the puzzle. Words are printed forward, backward, horizontally, vertically and diagonally.

3. Distribute crayons. Have the children color the pictures around the puzzle.

4. The answers to the puzzle are circled above.

Psalm 23 Word Search

O	V	E	R	F	L	O	W	S	D
P	A	S	T	U	R	E	S	R	L
E	N	T	O	I	V	E	E	O	M
L	O	A	I	F	N	H	R	W	A
B	I	F	L	D	P	D	O	R	G
A	N	F	O	E	L	L	E	W	D
T	T	O	H	Y	E	L	L	A	V
H	G	S	F	O	R	E	V	E	R
S	R	E	T	A	W	X	X	K	O

Words to Find:
ANOINT
DWELL
FOREVER
GOODNESS
LORD
OIL
OVERFLOWS
PASTURES
ROD
SHEPHERD
STAFF
TABLE
VALLEY
WATERS

The Lord is my shepherd, I shall not be in want. Psalm 23:1

Taste and See!

Memory Verse

Taste and see that the Lord is good; blessed is the man who takes refuge in him.
~Psalm 34:8

You Will Need:

* variety of food (see "Before Class")
* page 30, duplicated
* pencils or markers
* crayons

Before Class

1. Gather together several kinds of food of your choice. Try to include some of the children's favorites in addition to some foods that may be new to them.

2. Copy page 30 for each child.

Share and Discuss

Say, **Our memory verse today is a psalm. Many of the psalms were written by David as songs of praise to God. If you were going to write a psalm of praise to God, what would you say?** Let the children share some of the things for which they would like to thank God. Read the memory verse. Say, **David says that God has always been with him. Can you think of some special times in David's life when he depended on God?** Encourage the children to think about David as a young shepherd boy protecting his sheep against all kinds of dangers, and as the one God used to defeat the mighty giant, Goliath. Remind the children that David was chosen by God to be king over the people of Israel. Say, **Because he depended on God, David was a wise and mighty king. David faced many challenges in his life but he knew that God was with him through each one. David wrote about God's goodness to him in this psalm.**

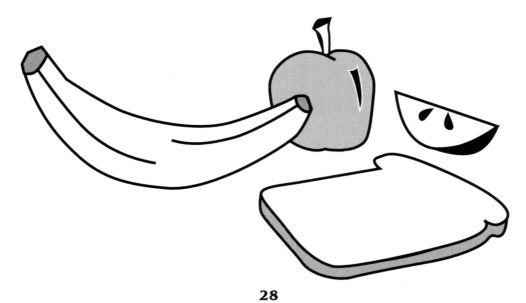

Edible Lesson:

1. Offer a blessing for the snack.

2. Say, **David was remembering all the ways God had taken care of him when he wrote "Taste and see that the Lord is good." What are some things that you can see that remind you of God's goodness?** Let the children respond. Then say, **As we prepare to enjoy our snack, let's think about some of the things that we can taste that remind us of God's goodness.**

3. Ask each child to name a food on the table, or another favorite food that God has given.

4. Enjoy your feast together, thanking God for His goodness.

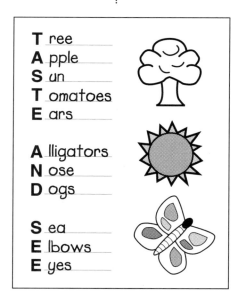

T ree
A pple
S un
T omatoes
E ars

A lligators
N ose
D ogs

S ea
E lbows
E yes

Activity: What Do You Taste and See?

1. Give each child a copy of page 30.

2. Distribute pencils or markers.

3. Help the children fill in the blanks by the letters TASTE AND SEE with something that God has given us to taste or see.

4. Distribute crayons. Encourage the children to decorate their sheets with pictures of things God has given us to enjoy.

—What Do You Taste and See?

Fill in the blanks with something good from God that begins with each letter.
Use the rest of the page to draw pictures of good things from God.

T _____

A _____

S _____

T _____

E _____

A _____

N _____

D _____

S _____

E _____

E _____

Taste and see that the Lord is good; blessed is the man who takes refuge in him. Psalm 34:8

The Apple of Your Eye

Memory Verse

Keep my commands and you will live; guard my teachings as the apple of your eye.
~Proverbs 7:2

You Will Need:

* apples, red and yellow
* patterns from p. 33
* felt, red, green and black
* glue
* ribbon, red
* index cards, cut in half

Before Class

1. Cut the apples into slices.

2. Leave some apples whole and place in a bowl for a centerpiece.

3. Use the patterns from page 33 to cut out one set of felt pieces for each child.

4. Cut the index cards in half.

Share and Discuss

Explain to the class that "the apple of your eye" is an expression referring to the pupil of one's eye. Have them look at the "apple" of their neighbor's eyes. Repeat the part of the memory verse that says "Guard my teachings as the apple of your eye." Ask, **What are some ways that we can guard our eyes? God gave us eyelids, eyelashes, tears and quick reflexes to keep our eyes from harmful intrusion, didn't He? And then we have created sunglasses and goggles to help protect them. What would happen to our eyesight if we did not have these things?** Allow time for responses. Have the children think of a time when they had something in their eyes. Ask, **How did it feel? As important as our eyes are to us, God's commandments are just as important and just as precious. We should keep God's commandments close to us.**

Edible Lesson:

1. Offer the blessing for the snack.

2. Say, **The apple of your eye is something that is very special to you. God's commandments to you are just as important. Let's have an apple snack to remind us of our precious eyes and God's precious commandments in His Word.**

3. Arrange the red and yellow apple slices on a plate.

4. Ask if anyone has noticed the "eye-appealing" arrangement of apples in the center of the table.

Activity: Apple Scripture Minder

1. Distribute a set of pre-cut felt pieces to each child.

2. Show how to glue the leaves and stem to the top of the apple.

3. Help the children glue the pouch piece on the front of the apple as shown in the illustration.

4. Show where to glue a ribbon on the back of the apple for hanging.

5. Talk with the children about their favorite Bible verses.

6. Distribute several index cards to each child.

7. Encourage the children to use the cards to record Bible verses that they want to remember and keep in their Apple Scripture Minder. Help them by looking up verses in the Bible and writing them on a chalkboard. Suggest verses for those who may be unfamiliar with the Bible.

Apple Scripture Minder

A Gentle Answer

Memory Verse

A gentle answer turns away wrath, but a harsh word stirs up anger. ~Proverbs 15:1

You Will Need:

* ✳ grapefruit
* ✳ knife
* ✳ bowl
* ✳ sugar
* ✳ page 36, duplicated
* ✳ pencils or markers
* ✳ crayons

Before Class

1. Slice grapefruit in a bowl. Do not add sugar.

2. Make a copy of page 36 for each child.

Share and Discuss

Begin by encouraging everyone to think about real-life situations in which the choice to say angry words resulted in anger from others. Likewise, ask if they can think of situations in which kind words resulted in kind actions from others. Encourage them to share their answers. It may be a new concept for your students that they have a choice how to respond in each situation. Say, **Each time you speak you can choose gentle or harsh words. But as the proverb clearly indicates, each choice carries its own set of consequences.**

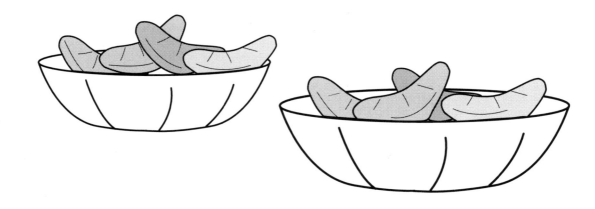

Edible Lesson:

1. Offer the blessing for the snack.

2. Say, **We can choose what kind of words we use. Our words can be kind and pleasing to God or harsh and hurtful to others and therefore not pleasing to God. Let's have a snack that will remind us of the types of answers God wants to come from our mouths.**

3. Have the children repeat this portion of the memory verse: "but a harsh word stirs up anger."

4. Give each child a bowl with grapefruit slices in it.

5. After the children taste the sour fruit, sprinkle sugar in each bowl.

6. Have the children taste the sweetened fruit. Say, **This one tastes better, doesn't it? Sweet words are always better.**

Prayer:

God, we thank You that we can choose the kinds of words we will speak. Help us that our words will always be like sweet fruit, not bitter. Amen.

That's OK. I didn't really like that doll anyway.

Bedtime!

Thanks for reminding me, Dad. I'm coming.

Activity: What Would You Say?

1. Give each child a copy of page 36 and a pencil or marker.

2. Talk about each picture.

3. Have the children think about the words they would say in each situation.

4. Help them write kind responses for the person speaking in each picture.

5. Distribute crayons and have the students color the pictures.

—What Would You Say? —

What might the child in each picture be saying? Help him or her choose a gentle answer by filling in the blanks. Color each picture.

A gentle answer turns away wrath, but a harsh word stirs up anger. Proverbs 15:1

Jesus Calls Some Fishermen

Memory Verse

"Come, follow me," Jesus said, "and I will make you fishers of men." ~Mark 1:17

You Will Need:

* brown sugar
* apple slices
* lemon juice
* small bowls
* page 39, duplicated
* crayons or markers

Before Class

1. Pour brown sugar in individual bowls for the children.

2. Soak the apple slices in lemon juice for five minutes, then drain.

3. Copy page 39 for each child.

Share and Discuss

Tell the story of Jesus walking along the Sea of Galilee and calling Peter, Andrew, James and John (Mark 1:16-20). Ask, **How did the disciples fish for fish? How do you fish for people?** Let the children respond. Remind the students that this is a story of Jesus' going fishing. His catch is the first disciples who left their nets to follow Him. Say, **Jesus has "caught" us with His love. We can "catch" others for Jesus by showing them His love as well.**

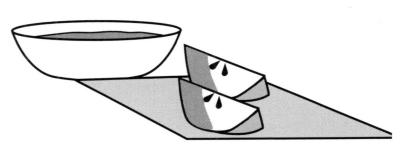

Edible Lesson:

1. Offer the blessing for the snack.

2. Say, **Jesus called the first disciples as He walked along the sandy shores of the Sea of Galilee. Our snack today reminds us of the sandy shore, where Jesus said to the disciples, "Follow me, and I will make you fishers of men."**

3. Give each child some apple slices and a bowl of brown sugar.

4. Have them dip the apples in the brown sugar "sand" before eating.

Prayer:

God, thank You for our snack that reminds us that Jesus walked along the shores of the Sea of Galilee, calling the fishermen to be His disciples. As we eat, help us remember that Jesus is calling us, too. Amen.

Activity: Fishers of Men

1. Give each child a copy of page 39.

2. Distribute crayons or markers.

3. Instruct the students to color the pictures that show ways that they will be fishers of men for Jesus.

4. Encourage the children to color all of the pictures. Help them to see that the illustrations show things that they can all do.

5. Have them write the memory verse on the bottom of their sheets before taking them home.

Fishers of Men

Which pictures show children being "fishers" for Jesus? Which can you do?

Living Water

Memory Verse

Whoever drinks the water I give him will never thirst. ~John 4:14

You Will Need:

* ✷ fruit
* ✷ bowls
* ✷ page 42, duplicated
* ✷ baby food jars
* ✷ potting soil
* ✷ small green plants
* ✷ heavy tape
* ✷ felt
* ✷ glue
* ✷ scissors

Before Class

1. Gather several types of melon or other fruit with a high water content.
2. Peel and slice the fruit into bite-sized pieces.
3. Trace the circle on page 42 onto felt and cut out one felt circle for each child.
4. Duplicate page 42 for each child.
5. Gather small plants, either from a nursery or grass and ferns from the yard.

Share and Discuss

When Jesus encountered the woman at the well (John 4:1-26), He described Himself and salvation as "living water." Say, **People of Israel understood living water to be water that is flowing and moving. Jesus was offering the woman the gift of eternal life — alive and forever moving and bubbling up in her heart.** Explain that Jesus knew that this woman was very empty inside because she had been married several times and was still unhappy. Say, **She was "thirsting" for something to make her life happy. Jesus wanted to give her the gift of Himself so that she would have peace and happiness in her life. Because the woman told her friends, many other people came to believe in Jesus and to receive the living water of His love.**

Edible Lesson:

1. Offer the blessing for the snack.

2. Say, **Jesus offered the woman the living water of His love. It wasn't the kind of water you drink, but the flood of Jesus' love that we feel inside. That is a wonderful feeling. Our snack today is filled with sweet water that will remind us of the sweetness of Jesus' love.**

3. Fill each child's bowl with fruit.

4. Talk about the water in the fruit and the sweetness of the water.

5. Discuss how wonderful water or juicy fruit tastes when we are thirsty.

Activity: Living Water Terrarium

1. Give each child a clean, empty jar.

2. Help the children fill their jars about half full with potting soil.

3. Give each child a plant. Help the children to push the root of the plant into the soil.

4. Help the children water the plants by moistening the soil. Be careful not to water them too much.

5. After the children have placed the lids on the terrariums, reinforce the lids with heavy tape.

6. Distribute scissors and copies of page 42. Have the children cut out the circle and glue it to the center of a pre-cut felt circle. Show how to set the terrarium in the center of the memory verse circle as a coaster.

7. Remind the children that they will never have to water their terrariums again. Say, **Just as your plant will never thirst for water, you will never thirst for Jesus' love and not be fulfilled. He is always there waiting for you.**

—**Living Water Terrarium** ————————

Whoever drinks the water I give him will never thirst. John 4:14

Miracle Seeds

Memory Verse

The secret of the kingdom of God has been given to you.
~Mark 4:11

You Will Need:

* ✱ pumpkin seeds
* ✱ sunflower seeds
* ✱ popcorn
* ✱ peanuts
* ✱ mustard seeds
* ✱ page 45, duplicated
* ✱ construction paper
* ✱ scissors
* ✱ glue
* ✱ crayons or markers

Before Class

1. Prepare the seeds, popcorn and peanuts in separate dishes. Pop some popcorn to eat but retain some unpopped seeds. Mustard seeds are found in the spice section at the grocery store.

2. Make a copy of page 45 for each child.

Share and Discuss

When Jesus wanted to teach about the kingdom, He turned to the power of the tiny seed. Show the children one of the seeds for the snack. Say, **What would happen if we planted this seed in a pot of good soil and gave it lots of water and sunshine?** Discuss the kind of plant that grows from that seed. Say, **God has placed something great inside a tiny seed. A seed doesn't look like anything at all on its own — but what wonderful things grow from seeds over time!** Show the children a single mustard seed. Review what Jesus says about this tiny seed (Matthew 13:31-32). Remind your children that God will help them to grow up to do great things for Him.

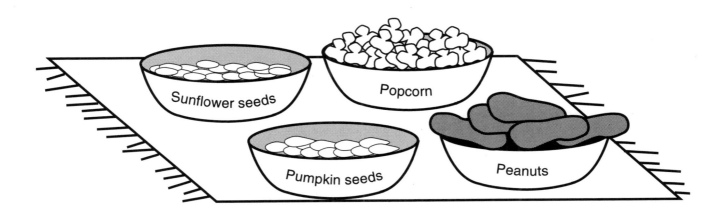

Sunflower seeds

Popcorn

Pumpkin seeds

Peanuts

Edible Lesson:

1. Offer the blessing for the snack.

2. Say, **Jesus used little seeds to teach us that the greatest things start small. Our snack today are seeds that we can eat.**

3. Introduce each bowl of edible seeds separately.

4. Let the children identify each seed and the plant or fruit that grows from it before they eat it.

Prayer:

God, thank You for the miracle seeds that You have filled with power and energy and that You provided for our snack today. As we eat, help us to think about Your Kingdom, and the wonderful things that we will grow up to do for You. Amen.

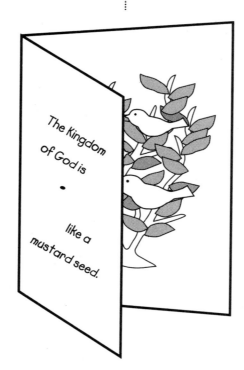

The Kingdom of God is • like a mustard seed.

Activity: Miracle Mustard Seed Card

1. Give each child a piece of construction paper and a copy of page 45.

2. Distribute scissors and glue and have the children cut out and glue their pictures on a folded sheet of construction paper.

3. Distribute crayons or markers and have the children color their pictures.

4. Give each child a single mustard seed to glue on the front of their card.

5. Help the children print on the front of their cards: "The Kingdom of God is like a mustard seed."

Miracle Mustard Seed Card

Salt the World with Love

Memory Verse

You are the salt of the earth.
~Matthew 5:13

You Will Need:

* ✳ cookbook
* ✳ crackers, salted and unsalted
* ✳ peanut butter
* ✳ spreaders or knives
* ✳ page 48, duplicated
* ✳ crayons or markers

Before Class

1. You will need both crackers with salt and those without salt.

2. Copy page 48 for each child.

Share and Discuss

Ask, **What does salt do? When do we use it?** Most children will think about the salt they put on food. Show the cookbook and read ingredient lists from some recipes. Ask, **Are you surprised that salt is an ingredient in most recipes? Did you think there would be salt in cookies and cakes?** Explain that the foods would not taste the same if the salt were left out. Say, **Salt is much more important in your life than you may know. Salt can be used as a medicine, like when you have a sore throat and gargle salt water. Our own bodies are made in part from salt — that's why tears and sweat taste salty! Jesus wants our Christian presence to be at work in the world the same way salt works. Just a little bit of salt makes everything around it better. We may not even be aware of its presence but we always know when it's absent. Salt makes a difference — just like Jesus and His love.**

Edible Lesson:

1. Offer the blessing for the snack.

2. Say, **Salt makes a difference in our food — it changes the taste from not-so-good to delicious. Jesus' love changes people from unhappy and angry to happy and filled with joy. Let's have a snack to remind us that Jesus wants us to be like salt, changing things with His love.**

3. Serve the unsalted crackers. Let the children comment on the snack.

4. Offer the crackers with salt. Ask, **What is the difference between these two snacks?**

5. Serve peanut butter to go on the crackers. Read the ingredients on the peanut butter aloud. Ask, **Is there salt in the peanut butter, too?**

Activity: Salt of the Earth

1. Distribute crayons or markers.

2. Give each child a copy of page 48.

3. Say, **Jesus needs you to share His love and let others know about Him.**

4. Discuss the pictures on the left side of the page.

5. Encourage the children to draw how they would be "salt" in each situation on the right side of the page. They should draw themselves helping the woman with her packages, inviting the child who is alone to play with them and reading to the little sister.

Salt of the Earth

The people in these pictures need someone to show them God's love. Draw yourself next to each picture, showing how you would be "salt" to them.

You are the salt of the earth. Matthew 5:13

Jesus Calms a Storm

Memory Verse

Where is your faith?
~Luke 8:25

You Will Need:

* limeade concentrate, one can
* pineapple juice, three cups
* lemon-lime drink, two quarts
* vanilla ice cream
* ice cream scoop
* punch bowl
* cups
* white paper
* page 51, duplicated
* crayons or markers
* scissors
* tape

Before Class

1. Wait to mix the drink until after the lesson. You may double or triple the drink recipe depending on the size of your class.

2. Copy page 51 for each child

Share and Discuss

Ask the children to close their eyes and imagine themselves as disciples with Jesus. Say, **It is night and you are out in a little boat on a big, wide lake. Suddenly a storm blows up on the lake. Big waves start to lash the sides of the boat, tossing it to and fro. But someone else is in the boat! Would you feel less afraid knowing that Jesus is in the boat with you? When Jesus was with the disciples He scolded the storm, and the wind and the water become calm and peaceful. Jesus is Lord over all, even God's creation. He is also Lord over those things that would frighten you as well.**

Edible Lesson:

1. Offer the blessing for the snack.

2. Say, **When Jesus calmed the storm at sea, it was a great miracle. Let's have a drink that will remind us of the stormy sea.**

3. In the punch bowl, combine the limeade concentrate, pineapple juice and lemon lime drink.

4. Add scoops of ice cream to the mixture to make the "foam."

5. Have the students recite the memory verse as you serve each cup.

Prayer:

God, we thank You for Jesus, who can even calm the stormy sea. Thank You for our snack today. Amen.

Activity: Magic Picture

1. Give each child a copy of page 51.

2. Distribute crayons or markers.

3. Have the children color all of the pictures on the sheet.

4. Distribute scissors. Help the children cut out all three pictures.

5. Have them lay the picture halves on top of the whole picture.

6. Show how to tape the halves onto the whole picture, taping only on the outside edges to form "hinges."

7. Demonstrate how to open the picture of the storm to see the picture of Jesus bringing calm to the sea.

Magic Picture

Where is your faith?
Luke 8:25

Give Us Each Day

Memory Verse

Give us each day our daily bread. ~Luke 11:3

You Will Need:

* variety of bread
* spreads
* baskets
* small plates
* plastic knives
* page 54, duplicated
* markers or crayons
* scissors
* construction paper
* glue

Before Class

1. Gather together a selection of breads that represent different cultures. Some ideas: tortillas, pita bread, matzo or scones. Include American-style white bread.

2. Also select several spreads such as butter or peanut butter.

3. Assemble and arrange the breads in baskets.

4. Copy page 54 for each child.

Share and Discuss

Pray the Lord's Prayer together. Ask, **Do you know who first gave us this prayer? Do you know that this is the prayer Jesus used to teach the disciples how to pray? What things are okay for us to pray about?** Let the children share. Say, **Jesus' prayer reminds us to ask God for all of the things that we need. Jesus knew we need forgiveness, love, protection, guidance and bread to eat for each day. Jesus shows us that God is our heavenly Father who loves us and cares about the needs of our bodies as well as our spirits.** Pray the Lord's Prayer together a second time.

Edible Lesson:

1. Offer the blessing for the snack.

2. Ask, **Why does Jesus say "bread" in His prayer?** Explain that bread is the most basic food in most cultures. Say, **Every country in the world has some type of bread in their diet. In many countries, people may only have bread to eat. We will have breads for our snack today.**

3. Introduce the breads one by one.

4. Talk about the country or region of origin for each bread.

5. Distribute the breads to each child and make the spreads available.

Prayer:

God, thank You that Jesus taught us how to pray. We thank You that You care about all of our needs. Thank You also for the bread You have provided for us today. Amen.

Give us each day our daily bread.

Luke 11:3

Activity: Daily Bread Table Reminder

1. Give each child a copy of page 54.

2. Distribute crayons or markers and have the children color the bread basket.

3. Distribute scissors and have the children cut out the bread basket.

4. Give each child a piece of construction paper.

5. Show the children how to fold the construction paper in half to make the table reminder.

6. Distribute glue. Have the children glue the bread basket to the front of the construction paper.

7. Help each child print the memory verse on the front of the table reminder.

8. Encourage the children to place their reminders on the table at family meal times to help them remember to pray to God and thank Him at each meal.

Daily Bread Table Reminder

Consider the Lilies

Memory Verse

Do not be afraid, little flock, for your Father has been pleased to give you the kingdom.
~Luke 12:32

You Will Need:

* vanilla yogurt
* peach slices, fresh or canned
* raisins
* bowls
* spoons
* page 57, duplicated
* crayons or markers

Before Class

1. Copy page 57 for each child.
2. Make a sample of the snack to show the class.
3. You may want to provide wet cloths for clean up because the children will be handling sticky peach slices.

Share and Discuss

Not even children are immune from worries and fears. Invite the students to share about things that cause them to worry or be afraid. Say, **Jesus knows that sometimes we are afraid. That is why He told us not to worry. God provides for all of the things we need. Have you ever seen a bird worrying about what it will wear or what it is going to eat? Why not? Have you ever seen a flower worrying about what it is going to put on? Why not? God knows exactly what each of us needs. God will take care of us.**

Edible Lesson:

1. Offer the blessing for the snack.

2. Say, **Jesus reminds us that lilies don't worry about what to wear** (Luke 12:27). **God cares for them. Our snack today will remind us that God cares for the flowers and that means He takes care of us.**

3. Spoon the yogurt into bowls.

4. Instruct the children to place two or three raisins in the center of their yogurt to make the center of the flower.

5. Distribute peach slices. Help the children place the slices around the raisins to make the flower petals.

Do not be afraid, little flock, for your Father has been pleased
to give you the kingdom. Luke 12:32

Activity: God Cares for You

1. Distribute crayons or markers.

2. Give each child a copy of page 57.

3. Have the children color the picture. Talk about the plants and animals in it. Ask, **What is missing in these things God cares for?** (them!)

4. Encourage the children to draw themselves in the picture.

5. Instruct them to memorize the verse at the bottom of their sheets when they take them home.

God Cares for You

Do not be afraid, little flock, for your Father has been pleased
to give you the kingdom. Luke 12:32

Good Fruit/Bad Fruit

Memory Verse

The good man brings good things out of the good stored up in him, and the evil man brings evil things out of the evil stored up in him.
~Matthew 12:35

You Will Need:

* ✴ fruit
* ✴ picture of a fruit tree
* ✴ two bowls
* ✴ page 60, duplicated
* ✴ crayons or markers
* ✴ tape
* ✴ construction paper

Before Class

1. You will need fresh fruit as well as bruised, spoiled or under-developed fruit for this lesson.
2. Find a picture of a fruit-bearing tree (or make your own using the illustration on page 60).
3. Arrange both kinds of fruit in separate bowls.
4. Prepare good fruit for the snack.
5. Copy page 60 for each child.

Share and Discuss

Say, **Jesus uses the imagery of a tree and its fruit to remind us that whatever is in our hearts — good or bad — cannot be concealed.** Show the picture of the fruit tree. Ask **Is this a healthy tree? How do we know?** Encourage the children to notice the green leaves and good fruit. Ask, **What if this were a sick or scrawny tree? What kind of fruit do you think it would have?** Let the children respond. Say, **Jesus taught us that we are like trees bearing fruit. Jesus said our fruit is what we do and what we say. He said that evil things inside of us produce bad fruit, but good things inside of us produce good fruit.**

Edible Lesson:

1. Offer the blessing for the snack.

2. Say, **Evil feelings inside of us produce bad fruit. What might we do and say when we feel angry or unhappy inside?** Let the children share. Say, **Having Jesus inside of us makes us happy and peaceful inside. What kind of good fruit comes out of us when we have Jesus in our hearts?** Let the children share. Say, **Our snack today reminds us that we can choose what fruit we want to have in our lives.**

3. Show the bowls of good and bad fruit.

4. Hold up the bad fruit for the children to see and smell.

5. Ask, **Is this what we want to have in our lives?**

6. Show the good fruit.

7. Ask the children which fruit they would like to eat for their snack.

8. Serve the good fruit. Comment on the sweet flavor and good smells.

Prayer:

God, thank You for our good, sweet fruit. Thank You for Jesus in our hearts, helping all our words and deeds to be good and kind and loving. In Jesus' name we pray. Amen.

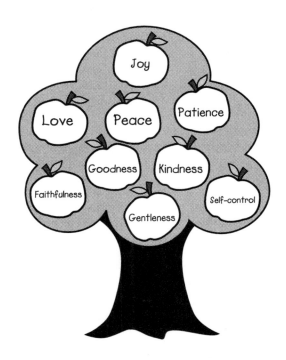

Activity: Fruit of the Spirit

1. Pass out crayons or markers.

2. Give each child a copy of page 60.

3. Have the children color the tree. Talk about how the tree is healthy and has a lot of good fruit.

4. Read Galatians 5:22-23. Say, **With Jesus in our hearts our words should be loving, kind, peaceful,** (etc.).

5. Help the children label the nine pieces of fruit on the tree with the nine fruits of the Spirit.

6. As they label each one, have the children name specific words and actions that are loving, kind, peaceful, etc.

7. Show how to tape the picture to construction paper for backing.

Fruit of the Spirit

The good man brings good things out of the good stored up in him, and the evil man brings evil things out of the evil stored up in him. Matthew 12:35

I Was Hungry

Memory Verse

Whatever you did for one of the least of these brothers of mine, you did for me.
~Matthew 25:40

You Will Need:

* ingredients for simple meal (see Before Class)
* page 63, duplicated
* crayons or markers
* scissors
* other decorations (see Activity)

Before Class

1. Gather together items for a meal the children may prepare, such as sandwiches.

2. Copy page 63 for each child.

Share and Discuss

Say, **Jesus told many special stories called parables in order to teach us about God and His Kingdom.** All children can identify with the scenario Jesus paints in Matthew 25:31-45 about the king returning to judge who was obedient and who was not. Ask, **What happens when your parents or teachers give you instructions and you do as you are told? What if you do not?** Explain that Jesus wants us to see that God is the king in the story. Say, **There will come a time when God will place all of those who have been obedient to Him on one side and all of those who have not on the other.** The most important question to ask the children is: **What did the obedient people do to obey God?** Help the children to see that obeying God includes taking care of those in need: the homeless, the sick, the imprisoned and the hungry. Say, **When we do something for someone in need, it is the very same thing as doing it for Jesus.** Have the children talk about what kind of meal they would prepare for Jesus.

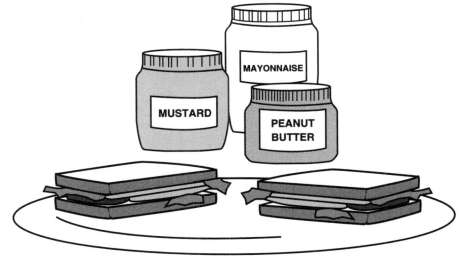

Edible Lesson:

1. Share the blessing for the snack.

2. Say, **We have a sandwich snack today which you will prepare. As you work on making the food for your own snack, be thinking about some ways that you can obey God.**

3. Give the children plenty of bread and sandwich spreads to make their snacks.

4. As they eat, talk with the children about those in your community who do not have such food to eat.

5. Suggest to the children that they can make a simple meal for someone in need.

6. Encourage the class to plan as many details as possible. Will the meal be for the homeless in a local soup kitchen? At your church? For the elderly in your community? What will the menu be? Will they have table decorations?

7. Remind the children that this is the same thing as inviting Jesus to a special meal. Repeat the memory verse.

8. Set a date and time for your special outreach meal.

Activity: Jesus Loves You Place Card

1. Give a copy of page 63 to each child.

2. Remind the children that the place cards they will make are special favors for their honored guests at the outreach meal.

3. Have the students cut out the place cards and fold them in half on the dashed line.

4. Distribute crayons or markers and any other items for decoration (glitter, sequins, yarn, etc.). Be sure they write JESUS LOVES YOU somewhere on the front of the place cards.

Jesus Loves You Place Card

Remember to Pray

Memory Verse

Paul and Silas were praying and singing hymns to God.
~Acts 16:25

You Will Need:

* pretzel twists
* page 66, duplicated
* glue
* ribbon
* construction paper

Before Class

1. Copy page 66 for each child.
2. You will need two types of pretzels for this lesson, both the traditional twists and salt-free twists.

Share and Discuss

Remind the students that Paul and Silas traveled to many places and told everyone about Jesus. Say, **Some people were glad to hear about Jesus, but some were not. Some people became very angry at Paul and Silas for talking about Jesus. Paul and Silas were arrested, beaten severely and thrown into prison. Do you think Paul and Silas stopped talking about Jesus? Do you think they forgot about God? Even though times were very bad for Paul and Silas, they praised God and prayed.** Remind the children that we should pray and praise God at all times — not just when things are going our way. Say, **God is always taking care of us. God was taking care of Paul and Silas.** Tell the rest of this remarkable story (Acts 16:16-40). Say, **Only God could bring about such a happy ending!**

Edible Lesson:

1. Say, **We should always remember to pray. Many centuries ago in Italy, some people decided to make a snack that would remind others to pray. They took dough and formed it in a shape of a person praying with his arms folded across his chest.** Demonstrate the stance. Ask, **Can you guess what that snack might be?**

2. Hold up a pretzel.

3. Have the children fold their arms across their chests "pretzel-style" as you join in the blessing.

4. Serve the pretzels.

Prayer:

God, thank You for always taking care of us. We thank You for our pretzels as a reminder that we can always pray to You. In Jesus' name we pray. Amen.

Activity: Pretzel Prayer Reminder

1. Distribute the small, salt-free pretzels, glue and a copy of page 66 to each child.

2. Show how to cut out and trace the heart on construction paper and cut it out.

3. Show how to arrange the pretzels inside the white paper heart. Have the students carefully glue the pretzels to the paper.

4. Help them to tie a piece of ribbon into a bow and glue it to the top of the pretzel heart.

5. Allow to dry.

6. Have the children glue the construction paper heart on the back of the pretzel heart for stability.

7. Show where to glue a length of ribbon on the back for hanging.

Pretzel Prayer Reminder

Love Is the Greatest

special day: Valentine's Day

Memory Verse

Faith, hope and love...the greatest of these is love.
~1 Corinthians 13:13

You Will Need:

* heart-shaped cookie cutter
* knife
* crackers
* dried beef, two packages
* cream cheese, two 8 oz. packages
* page 69, duplicated
* scissors
* construction paper
* tape
* crayons or markers

Before Class

1. Chop the dried beef into fine pieces. You may want to unwrap the cream cheese and allow it to soften during the lesson.

2. Copy page 69 for each child.

Share and Discuss

Ask, **What is love?** Let the children share their ideas. Remind them to think about their experiences of the love of family, friends and God. Read Paul's description of love to the class (1 Corinthians 13:4-8). Say, **Paul said, "I can do many wonderful things — but if I am not loving, I am nothing."** Ask, **Do you know someone who never seems to be loving and kind?** Help the children to understand that people who are unloving are usually people who feel that no one loves them. Help the children think about ways that they can give love to those who need it.

Edible Lesson:

1. Offer the blessing for the snack.

2. Say, **Paul taught us that love is the greatest of all.** Show a heart-shaped cookie cutter. Discuss the meaning of the heart as a symbol of love. Say, **Today our snack will be heart-shaped to remind us of love.**

3. Unwrap and place the two cakes of cream cheese on a plate, side-by-side.

4. When they are softened, press the heart-shaped cookie cutter into the center of the cream cheese to make a heart-shaped impression. Do not try to cut through the cream cheese with the cookie cutter.

5. Use a knife to cut around the heart-shaped impression.

6. Cover the outside of the heart with the dried beef.

7. Serve as a spread with crackers.

Activity: Love Card

1. Give each child a piece of construction paper to make the outside of the card.

2. Have the children fold the construction paper in half so the card opens on the side.

3. Distribute crayons or markers.

4. Help the children print on the front of the cards, "Faith, Hope, Love...the greatest of these is..."

5. Give each child a copy of page 69.

6. Have the children color the heart and write "love!" in big letters on it.

7. Distribute scissors for the children to cut out the heart and the mounting piece from the pattern sheet.

8. Show how to fold the mounting piece along the dotted lines, accordion-style.

9. Show the children how to make a loop of tape and secure the heart to the mounting piece.

10. They should tape the other end of the mounting piece to the inside right page of the card.

11. Show the children how to make sure that the heart and mounting piece are flat against the back of the card before closing.

12. Encourage the children to share their card with someone who needs to know God's love.

Love Card

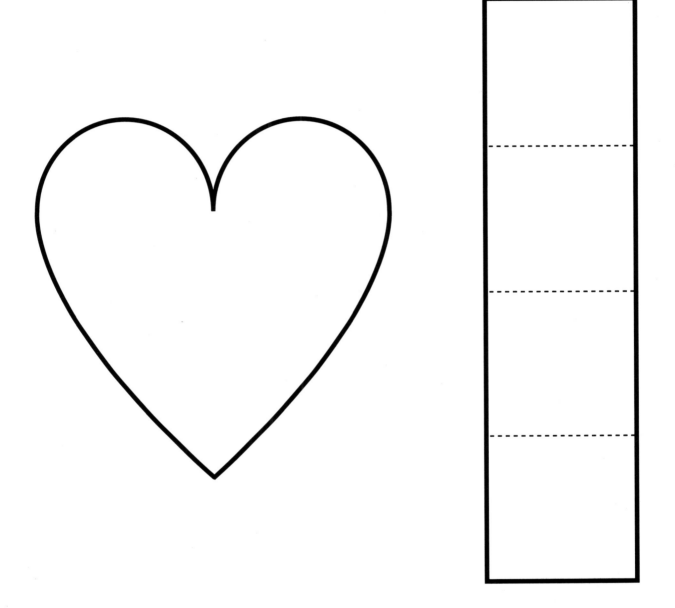

Jesus Died for You

Memory Verse

While we were still sinners, Christ died for us.
~Romans 5:8

You Will Need:

* ✳ cross
* ✳ cookie dough
* ✳ decorator icing
* ✳ baking sheets
* ✳ oven
* ✳ page 72, duplicated
* ✳ scissors
* ✳ tape
* ✳ crayons or markers

Before Class

1. Gather ingredients for a favorite cookie recipe or purchase prepared cookie dough.

2. Copy page 72 twice for each child.

Share and Discuss

Lent is the 40-day period before Easter and a special time of focus on all that Christ has done for us. This is a wonderful opportunity to discuss with your class the true meaning of the events of Holy Week and Easter. Begin by showing the children a cross. Ask, **Why is the cross important? Why do we have so many crosses in our church?** Let the children share. Say, **Jesus died on the cross for our sins**. Ask the children what "sins" are. Explain that sins are anything we do that disobeys God. Let the children think about things in their lives that are sins. Explain that we all sin, but Jesus died on the cross so that we could ask God to forgive us when we sin. Say, **We all make mistakes and sin, but we can tell God that we are sorry. We can ask Him to help us not to make that mistake again.** Older children may want to know why Jesus had to die for our sins. To explain, ask the children what happens at their house when they do something wrong. All children can identify with being punished. Say, **God allowed Jesus to take the punishment for our sins. Christ lovingly died on the cross for each one of us.** Conclude by going around the room and saying, "Christ died for [name]" as you hold up the cross.

Edible Lesson:

1. Offer the blessing for the snack.

2. Say, **We love the cross because it reminds us that Jesus died for our sins. We have crosses in the church. We wear crosses around our necks. Today we will put a cross on our snack to honor Jesus.**

3. Prepare the cookies according to the recipe or package directions.

4. Help the children make a cross on their cookies with icing. (This is a simple version of the traditional Lenten hot cross buns: a sweet bun with an icing cross on top.)

Prayer:

God, thank You for Jesus and His love. We thank You for the cross represented on our snack. As we eat, help us to remember that Jesus loved us so much He died on the cross for us. Amen.

Activity: Cross Reminder Card

1. Give each child one copy of page 72.

2. Distribute crayons or markers and scissors.

3. Help the children print the words "Christ" and "died" on the cross. The two words should make a cross shape, intersecting at "i."

4. Have the children cut out their crosses.

5. Distribute the second copy of page 72.

6. Help the children print the words "for" and "you" on this cross in the same intersecting fashion. The two words should meet at "o."

7. They should not cut this cross out. Encourage the children to color and decorate the area around it.

8. Distribute tape.

9. Help the children tape the first cross directly over the top of the second cross. They should tape only at the top of the card so that the top cross can be lifted to reveal the message on the bottom cross.

10. Tell the students they may present the cross card to someone who needs to be reminded of Christ's gift of life to us.

Cross Reminder Card

Hosanna!

special day: Palm Sunday

Memory Verse

"Hosanna!" "Blessed is he who comes in the name of the Lord." ~Mark 11:9

You Will Need:

* pan, 9"x13"
* aluminum foil
* graham crackers
* saucepan
* cook top and oven
* margarine or butter, one stick
* brown sugar, ½ cup
* nuts, one cup
* page 75, duplicated
* craft sticks
* crayons or markers
* scissors
* tape
* glue
* construction paper

Before Class

1. You may either make the Jerusalem's Road Treats before class or have the students assist you in making them.
2. Copy page 75 for each child.

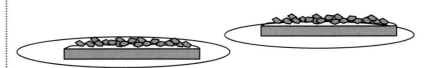

Share and Discuss

As you tell the story of Jesus' triumphant entry into the city of Jerusalem (Mark 11:1-11), capture all of the drama and excitement of the scene. Say, **Jesus stood on the Mount of Olives, looking down on the city. He directed His disciples to borrow a young donkey to carry Him. As Jesus rode into the city, people showed that they adored Him by laying down branches and even their cloaks on the road for Him to ride over. This is the kind of treatment that people customarily gave to royalty. They saw Jesus as their King.** Encourage the children to imagine that they were a part of this wonderful day. Ask, **What would you do and say to Jesus as He passed by?** Explain that the people shouted "Hosanna," a Hebrew word that means "save." Ask, **What do kings do?** Explain that the people thought Jesus was going to be a king who would sit on a throne and rule over them. Say, **They didn't understand that Jesus was going to show them His love and guidance by dying on the cross for their sins. They also didn't know that God would raise Him from the dead on Easter to be their heavenly King.**

Edible Lesson:

1. Offer the blessing for the snack.

2. Say, **As Jesus entered into the city of Jerusalem riding on a donkey, the people stood along the road, spreading their cloaks and branches to honor Him. As we eat our snack today, let's remember how Jesus willingly followed the road into Jerusalem to die for us.**

3. Line the pan with the foil.

4. Place a layer of graham crackers along the bottom of the pan.

5. Mix the butter, brown sugar and nuts in a saucepan and boil for three minutes.

6. Pour the mixture over the graham crackers and bake for 11 minutes at 325 degrees.

7. When the treats are cool, lift the foil out of the pan. Break the crackers into serving-sized pieces.

Prayer:

God, thank You that Jesus went into Jerusalem to die for us. As we eat our snack help us to remember the people who lined the road as Jesus passed by. Help us, God, to praise Jesus as our King also. Amen.

Activity: Triumphal Entry Action Picture

1. Give each child a copy of page 75 and crayons or markers.

2. Discuss the pictures on the activity sheet and explain their significance to the Palm Sunday story.

3. Have the children color and cut out the pictures.

4. Show how to tape a craft stick to the back of the picture of Jesus riding the donkey.

5. Instruct the students to glue the pictures of the road and the crowds to a piece of construction paper. They should glue the crowd toward the left of the road.

6. Have the children cut on the dotted line on the road to make a slit (fold the paper slightly while cutting).

7. Show how to make Jesus "ride" into Jerusalem by inserting the craft stick in the slit on the road and holding it from behind. Move the picture along the slit in the road toward the people.

Triumphal Entry Action Picture

"Hosanna!" "Blessed is he who comes in the name of the Lord."
Mark 11:9

He Is Risen!

special day: Easter

Memory Verse

He is not here; he has risen!
-Luke 24:6

You Will Need:

* eggs
* milk
* bowl
* whisk
* American cheese slices
* custard cups
* English muffins
* microwave oven
* page 78, duplicated
* scissors
* construction paper
* glue
* crayons or markers

Before Class

1. You may make the snacks just before class or have the students assist you in making them.

2. Copy page 78 for each child.

Share and Discuss

The story of the first Easter is a wonderful story of sadness turned to joy; hopeless to hope; death to eternal life. Review the story of Jesus' suffering and death with the class. Remind the children that the women were still sad because they thought Jesus was dead and they would never see Him again. Say, **Jesus is risen and He is alive today and forever! Because He lives, we will live forever in heaven with Him. Each time we come together to worship is a "little Easter," a time for thanking God for raising Jesus from the dead.**

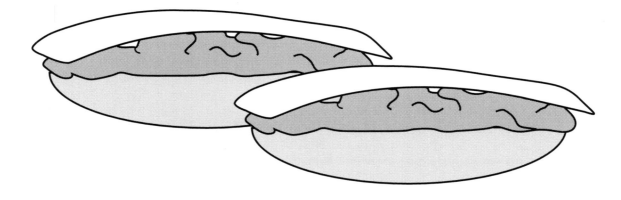

Edible Lesson:

1. Offer the blessing for the snack.
2. Say, **The women came to Jesus' tomb that morning just as the sun was coming up. There, in the light of dawn, they saw that the stone was rolled away and Jesus was gone. The angels told them, "He is not here, he has risen." Let's celebrate Jesus' resurrection with a snack that reminds us of sunrise.**
3. In a bowl, break the eggs.
4. Whisk the eggs with a small amount of milk.
5. Microwave the egg mixture in custard cups until firm.
6. Turn out onto English muffin halves.
7. Place a slice of American cheese on top before serving.

Prayer:

God, thank You for that Easter long ago when the women found the tomb empty and the angels said that Jesus was alive. What a sunrise that must have been! Help us to live for You. In Jesus name we pray. Amen.

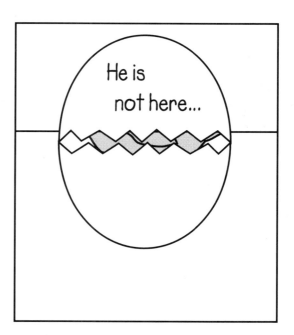

Activity: Easter Surprise Card

1. Give each child a copy of page 78.
2. Distribute crayons or markers and have the children color the chick and egg shell halves.
3. Distribute scissors and have the children cut out the figures.
4. Give each child a piece of construction paper for their card. Lay the paper on the table with the longer length vertical.
5. Help each child glue the bottom half of their egg shell and the chick (as if sitting in the shell) to the bottom third of their paper.
6. Show how to print, "He is risen!" over the chick.
7. Instruct the students to fold the top edge of the paper down to meet the top edge of the egg shell.
8. Help the children glue the top half of the egg shell to the front of the folded part of the paper. Show how to make the two egg-shell halves meet to form a whole egg.
9. Show where to print the words "He is not here..." above the egg on the top of the page.
10. Open the card to see the chick come out of the egg!

Easter Surprise Card

How the Church Was Born

special day: Pentecost

Memory Verse

When the day of Pentecost came, they were all together in one place. ~Acts 2:1

You Will Need:

* cupcakes
* red birthday candles
* matches or lighter
* page 81, duplicated
* red crepe paper
* tape
* crayons or markers
* string

Before Class

1. Prepare or purchase cupcakes.

2. Make a copy of page 81 for each child.

Share and Discuss

Ask, **When is your birthday?** Allow time for answers. Then ask, **Did you know that the church has a birthday? This is the story of how the church was born.** Read Acts 2:1-12, 14, 22-24 and 38-41. Explain that Jesus had instructed His followers to wait for He would do something wonderful. Say, **That wonderful thing was the gift of the Holy Spirit.** Emphasize that the Holy Spirit came to the people as wind and flame. Say, **When Jesus gave the people the gift of the Holy Spirit, they began to speak in other languages so that every person, regardless of the language they spoke, could understand what was being said. There were many people in Jerusalem who did not know that Jesus was God's Son. When the people began asking what was happening, Peter had an opportunity to tell them about Jesus and how He had died on the cross for the sins of everyone. Many of the people hearing Peter realized that they needed to be forgiven of their sins and start following Jesus. That very day 3,000 people repented of their sins and were baptized. The church started to grow on the day of its birth when the Holy Spirit came to give it life.**

Edible Lesson:

1. Offer the blessing for the snack.

2. Say, **Jesus sent His Holy Spirit to the people. That is how the church was born. How did the people know the Spirit was present?** Encourage the students to understand the presence of the Holy Spirit as wind and fire. Say, **Our snack today is a symbol of the Holy Spirit and the birth of the church.**

3. Distribute the cupcakes.

4. Say, **Our cupcakes are little birthday cakes for the church. Each of us has one because we are the church! The church is God's people together following Jesus.**

5. Distribute red candles.

6. Light each child's candle.

7. Talk about how the Holy Spirit came to the people as little flames of fire.

8. Say, **The Holy Spirit sounded like the rush of wind. Listen to what it sounds like when we blow out our candles together.** Then have the children blow out their candles at one time.

Prayer:

God, thank You for the Church and for our birthday celebration today. We thank You for the flame on our cupcakes and for our own breath as reminders that the Holy Spirit is with us always. Bless our food, we pray. In Jesus' name. Amen.

Activity: Pentecost Wind Catcher

1. Give each child a copy of page 81.

2. Distribute crayons or markers and encourage the children to color the illustration in fiery reds and oranges. Have them write "Come Holy Spirit" above the dove.

3. Help them to roll their sheets lengthwise and tape them right at the edges.

4. Distribute crepe paper.

5. Show how to tape the streamers to the bottom of the wind catcher below the flames and how to tape lengths of string to four spots at the top of the wind catcher.

6. Go around and tie the four strings together at the top of each child's wind catcher. Leave a length of string long enough to form a loop for hanging.

Pentecost Wind Catcher

Working and Resting for God

special day: Labor Day

Memory Verse

Six days you shall labor and do all your work, but the seventh day is a Sabbath to the Lord your God. ~Exodus 20:9-10

You Will Need:

* flavored gelatin
* clear, plastic gloves
* rubber bands or string
* trays
* page 84, duplicated
* finger paint
* shallow, flat dishes
* construction paper
* glue or tape
* string
* paper towels or hand wipes
* old newspapers

Before Class

1. Purchase clear, plastic gloves from a discount or restaurant supply store.

2. Prepare gelatin according to package directions. Use slightly less water to give the gelatin stronger texture.

3. Pour the gelatin mixture into the plastic gloves. Fasten the gloves tightly closed with rubber bands or string.

4. Lay the gelatin hands flat on a tray and refrigerate for at least three hours or until very firm.

5. Copy page 84 once for each child.

Share and Discuss

Say, **Long ago, God gave Moses and the children of Israel ten special laws called "The Ten Commandments." God gave us these commandments to teach us how He wants us to live.** Read the fourth commandment concerning the Sabbath Day. Say, **The Sabbath is a day of rest from work — a day that is spent worshipping God instead.** Ask, **What day of the week is our Sabbath?** Say, **Labor Day is a day our nation sets aside from work to be thankful. As God's children, how do we show our thanks to Him?** Let the children share. Encourage them to see that we thank God by keeping His commandment to do good work for six days and set the seventh day aside for rest and worship.

Edible Lesson:

1. Offer the blessing for the snack. Encourage each child to fold their hands in prayer as they say thanks for the snack.

2. Hold up your hands. Say, **For six days God gives us strength and the ability to use our hands in work.** Let the children name some of the work we do with our hands. Say, **On the seventh day, what does God want us to do?** Let the children share. Fold your hands as if in prayer to encourage the children to associate the day of rest as an important day of worship. Say, **We use our hands to work for six days. On the seventh day we use our hands to worship God as we rest from our work. Our snack today reminds us that we can use our hands for God every day.**

3. Help the children carefully remove the plastic covering from their gelatin hands.

Prayer:

God, thank You that You have given us hands to work for You and to worship You. Thank You for our snack. May we remember always to use our hands for You. Amen.

I Give My Hands to God

Six days you shall labor and do all your work, but the seventh day is a Sabbath to the Lord your God.
Exodus 20:9-10

Activity: Hands for God Poster

1. Cover the work surface with old newspapers.

2. Give each child a copy of page 84.

3. Show how to glue or tape the page onto construction paper for backing.

4. Pour finger paint into shallow flat dishes.

5. Help each child make their hand prints on the poster with the paint.

6. Have hand wipes or paper towels on hand for clean-up.

7. Show where to fasten a length of string on the back of the poster for hanging.

I Give My Hands to God

Six days you shall labor and do all your work, but the seventh day is a Sabbath to the Lord your God.

Exodus 20:9-10

Thank You, Lord

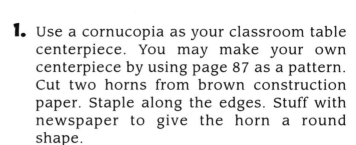

special day: Thanksgiving

Memory Verse

Great is the Lord and most worthy of praise.
~Psalm 145:3

You Will Need:

* ice cream cones, pointed ends
* vanilla yogurt
* fresh fruit
* knife
* bowls
* spoons
* cornucopia
* page 87, duplicated
* crayons or markers

Before Class

1. Use a cornucopia as your classroom table centerpiece. You may make your own centerpiece by using page 87 as a pattern. Cut two horns from brown construction paper. Staple along the edges. Stuff with newspaper to give the horn a round shape.

2. Arrange fresh fruit (apples, bananas, oranges, etc.), as if it is coming out of the cornucopia.

3. Slice and peel extra fruit for eating.

4. Pour yogurt in a bowl.

Share and Discuss

Say, **Thanksgiving is a special time for thanking God. Let's pretend that we are going to write a song to say "thank You" to God for all He has done for us.** Let the children share things that they would like to put in their thank-you song. Turn in your Bible to the Psalms. Explain that people long ago wrote many thank-you songs, or "psalms," to God. Share Psalm 145 with the children. Let them comment on what they have heard. As you discuss, try to draw parallels between Psalm 145 and the "thank-you's" that the children suggested for their own song. Say, **Just like the psalmist, we want to thank God because He loves us and supplies all our needs — not just at Thanksgiving, but every day of the year.**

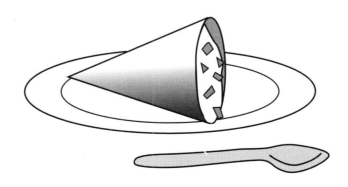

Edible Lesson:

1. Offer the blessing for the snack.

2. Say, **At Thanksgiving, one symbol of God's blessings is a cornucopia.** Talk with the children about the centerpiece. Have fruit and other items symbolic of God's blessings (Bible, picture of church, cross, etc.) for the children to add to the display. Say, **God has given us so much to be thankful for. Today, our snack will remind us to be thankful.**

3. Give each child an ice cream cone "cornucopia."

4. Have on hand bowls of yogurt and sliced fresh fruit.

5. Let the children spoon the food into their ice cream cones.

6. Provide spoons to make eating easier.

Prayer:

God, thank You for Thanksgiving as a special time to say "thank You" for all that You have done for us. Lord, help us to remember to say "thank You" every day. In Jesus' name we pray. Amen.

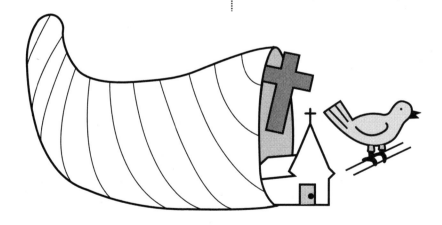

Great is the Lord and most worthy of praise. Psalm 145:3

Activity: Thank You, God

1. Distribute crayons or markers.

2. Give each child a copy of page 87.

3. Encourage the children to color the cornucopia and fill it to overflowing by drawing the things for which they are most thankful (food, church, family, etc.).

4. Remind them to memorize the verse underneath the cornucopia after taking the sheet home.

—Thank You, God —————

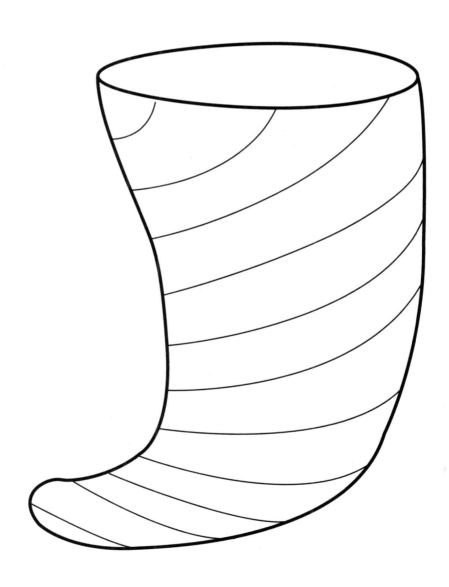

Great is the Lord and most worthy of praise. Psalm 145:3

God's Prophecy

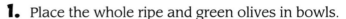

special day: Advent

Memory Verse

A shoot will come up from the stump of Jesse...The Spirit of the Lord will rest on him.
~Isaiah 11:1-2

You Will Need:

* olive tree picture
* green olives, pitted
* ripe olives, pitted
* bowls
* cream cheese
* crackers or bread
* knife
* small plates or napkins
* page 90, duplicated
* drawing paper
* crayons or markers
* Christmas stickers
* scissors
* tape
* string

Before Class

1. Place the whole ripe and green olives in bowls.

2. Chop extra olives for the cream cheese spread (see Edible Lesson).

3. Consult a Bible dictionary or visit a library to locate a picture of an olive tree.

4. Make two copies of page 90 for each child. On one copy, make a start cut on the dashed line of each square with scissors or a craft knife so the children can cut around them easier.

Share and Discuss

Say, **Many centuries before the birth of Christ, God spoke to the prophet Isaiah of the coming Messiah.** Read Isaiah 11:1-9 to the class. Say, **Isaiah is telling the people about God's promise of Jesus. God's people in Isaiah's day needed to know that God loved them. They had disobeyed God. Someone else had taken their land. Now they were back in their homeland again, but everything, including the temple, was in ruins. God sent them this message of good news.** As you discuss the description of the Messiah with the children, have them compare Isaiah's words with what they know about Jesus. Draw the children's attention to verse one and show the picture of the olive tree. Say, **Everyone in Israel knew about olive trees. If an olive tree is chopped down, it does not die — a new shoot will grow out of the stump. Isaiah is saying that Jesus is going to come from the family of Jesse. Jesse was the father of King David. Both Mary and Joseph were descendants of David. We celebrate Advent as a time of waiting and preparing for the coming of Christmas Day and Jesus' birth.**

Edible Lesson:

1. Offer the blessing for the snack.

2. Say, **Just as Isaiah used the olive tree to explain how God would one day send His Son, we will have olives for our snack to remind us that God was true to His promise. He sent us Jesus!**

3. Show the children the bowls of green and ripe olives.

4. Encourage them to taste both kinds of olives. Explain that olives were an important food to the people of Israel in Bible times and yet today.

5. Spread bread or crackers with cream cheese. Provide chopped olives for those who want them on their snack.

Prayer:

God, thank You that long ago You told Your people about the coming of Christ. We thank You for Isaiah who used the olive tree to show the people what You were going to do. And we thank You for our snack today as a reminder that Jesus has come, just as You promised. Amen.

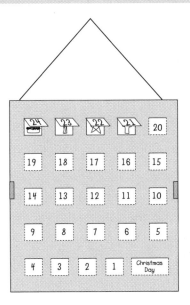

Activity: Advent Calendar

1. Discuss with the children that Advent is a time of waiting and preparing for the birth of Jesus.

2. Give each child one copy of page 90. Distribute crayons or markers and Christmas stickers.

3. Have the children draw a small picture or place a sticker inside each of the small squares on one sheet of the Advent calendar pattern. Encourage them to draw pictures that relate to Jesus' birth.

4. Encourage the children to use the last, large square to draw a special surprise picture showing the birth of Jesus.

5. Give the children the second copy of page 90.

6. Have them number the squares 1-24, beginning with 24 at the top left and continuing row by row. They should label the large square "Christmas Day."

7. Help the children cut around each of the squares on the dashed lines by inserting their scissors where you made cuts. Emphasize that they should not cut the tops of the squares.

8. Lay this sheet over the one with pictures. Show how to gently lift the flaps of the top sheet to make sure that the two sheets are properly aligned, then close the flaps again.

9. Help the children tape the sheets together around the edges.

10. Tape a length of string to the backs of the calendars for hanging.

Advent Calender

Born in a Manger

special day: Christmas

Memory Verse

She wrapped him in cloths and placed him in a manger, because there was no room for them in the inn. ~Luke 2:7

You Will Need:

* hot dogs
* canned biscuits
* rolling pin (optional)
* knife
* cookie sheet
* oven
* page 93, duplicated
* drawing paper
* crayons or markers
* glue
* scissors
* straw (optional)
* string

Before Class

1. Cut the hot dogs into thirds.
2. Copy page 93 for each child.

Share and Discuss

A striking element of the first Christmas is the humble circumstances surrounding Jesus' birth. Caesar Augustus — ruler of the Roman world and powerful enough to order everyone to travel long distances to their place of birth — had great earthly influence and wealth. Jesus, in contrast, was born in the poorest of circumstances, but He is the Son of God! Jesus was born in a stable instead of a palace. To the many people of the earth who are excluded from palaces, God sent His Son, Jesus. As you teach this Christmas lesson, help the children to see the contrast between rich and poor. Ask, **Have you ever known someone who felt important because of his or her possessions or social status?** Help the children to see that Jesus, born humbly, is God's gift to everyone — rich and poor alike.

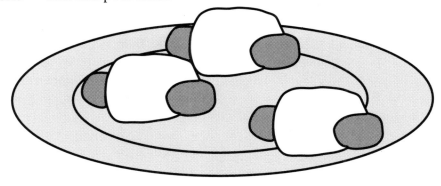

Edible Lesson:

1. Offer the blessing for the snack.

2. Say, **Mary and Joseph were not wealthy. They could not afford elaborate blankets so they wrapped Jesus in strips of cloth to keep Him warm. Our snack today will remind us of Jesus' "swaddling clothes."**

3. Have the children flatten out the biscuits slightly with their hands or a rolling pin. Do not over-flatten.

4. Cut the biscuits in half.

5. Help the children wrap the hot dogs in the strips of biscuit dough.

6. Place the snacks on a cookie sheet. Bake at 375 degrees until the biscuit strips are golden brown. Serve and enjoy!

Prayer:

God, we are all important to You, no matter where we were born, how much money we have or the color of our skin. Thank You for loving us enough to send Jesus. Amen.

She wrapped him in cloths and placed him in a manger, because there was no room for them in the inn. Luke 2:7

Activity: Make-It-Yourself Nativity

1. Give each child one copy of page 93.

2. Distribute crayons or markers for coloring the figures.

3. Give each child a piece of drawing paper.

4. Have the children draw an empty stable on their paper.

5. Distribute scissors.

6. Let the children cut out their nativity scene figures and glue them onto their stable picture.

7. Have the children write the memory verse above the picture.

8. If you have straw, encourage the children to glue pieces to their manger scene.

9. Show how to glue string to the back of the picture for hanging.

Make-It-Yourself Nativity

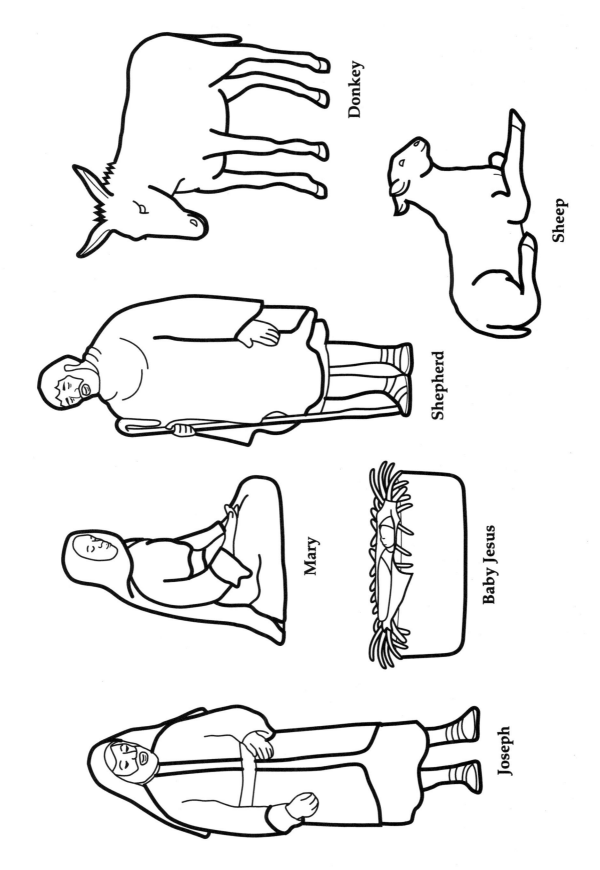

Donkey

Sheep

Shepherd

Mary

Baby Jesus

Joseph

Follow His Star

special day: Epiphany

Memory Verse

We saw his star in the east and have come to worship him.
~Matthew 2:2

You Will Need:

* ✳ butter, one cup
* ✳ vanilla, one teaspoon
* ✳ flour, 2⅓ cups
* ✳ egg
* ✳ mixing bowl
* ✳ powdered sugar
* ✳ chocolate kisses, one package
* ✳ microwave oven
* ✳ shoe box with lid
* ✳ foil, silver or gold
* ✳ waxed paper
* ✳ page 96, duplicated
* ✳ pencils or markers
* ✳ crayons

Before Class

1. If your classroom is not accessible to a microwave oven, prepare the snack before the lesson.

2. Make a treasure box for the snack nuggets by covering the box with foil. Line the box with waxed paper.

3. Copy page 96 for each child.

Share and Discuss

Most children are familiar with the story of the wise men following the star to the Holy Family. It may be new information to your children that not everyone was happy about the birth of Jesus. Explain that Herod was so jealous of Jesus that he wanted to harm him. Say, **Herod was a wicked man who would do anything to get rid of anyone more powerful than he. Herod plotted his evil plan. He lied to the wise men so they would return and tell him where Jesus was.** Help the children to see that the wise men had a choice: they could listen to Herod or to God. Conclude by highlighting the obedience of the wise men to God. Say, **They followed God's star to the place where Mary, Joseph and baby Jesus were. When God warned them in a dream not to return to Herod, they listened to God and returned home by another route.**

Edible Lesson:

1. Offer the blessing for the snack.

2. Say, **The wise men followed the star to the place where Jesus was. They were so thankful to see Him that they opened their treasures and gave Jesus the most precious gifts they had. As we make and enjoy our Treasure Nuggets, we can remember to give thanks for Jesus.**

3. The students may assist you on any or all of the recipe steps.

4. Microwave the butter until it is softened.

5. Beat in the egg, vanilla and a $1/2$-cup of the powdered sugar until fluffy.

6. Blend in flour to make dough.

7. Shape the nuggets by wrapping one teaspoon of dough around one chocolate kiss.

8. Microwave the nuggets on low for about five minutes or until no longer doughy.

9. Roll the nuggets in powdered sugar.

10. Place the nuggets in the treasure box for serving.

Prayer:

God, thank You for the wise men who followed Your star to baby Jesus and gave Him their treasures. Most of all we thank You for Jesus. As we eat our treasure snacks, may we remember to give our best to Jesus. Amen.

Activity: Follow His Star Puzzle

1. Distribute a copy of the "Follow His Star" puzzle from page 96 to each child.

2. Discuss the clues and help the children complete the puzzle (see answers above).

3. Have them color the pictures before taking it home. Encourage them to memorize the verse on the bottom.

Follow His Star Puzzle

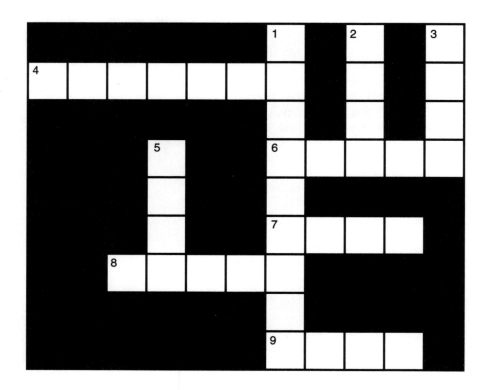

Across

4. Gift for baby Jesus; it burns (Matthew 2:11)

6. Evil king (Matthew 2:1)

7. Where the star was (Matthew 2:2)

8. Gift for baby Jesus; it smells good (Matthew 2:11)

9. The wise men (Matthew 2:1)

Down

1. Where Jesus was born (Matthew 2:1)

2. The magi followed it (Matthew 2:2)

3. Gift for baby Jesus; we make jewelry from it (Matthew 2:11)

5. Jesus' mother (Matthew 1:18)

We saw his star in the east and have come to worship him. ~Matthew 2:2